HUNGERPOTS

HESTER
KNIBBE

HUNGERPOTS

NEW & SELECTED POEMS

TRANSLATED BY
JACQUELYN POPE

 EYEWEAR PUBLISHING

First published in 2015
by Eyewear Publishing Ltd
74 Leith Mansions, Grantully Road
London w9 1lj
United Kingdom

Typeset with graphic design by Edwin Smet
Printed in England by TJ International Ltd, Padstow, Cornwall

© 2015 Hester Knibbe
© 2015 Jacquelyn Pope, Translation and introduction
Published in 2009, 2011, 2014 by De Arbeiderspers, Amsterdam

ISBN 978-1-908998-80-4

*Eyewear wishes to thank Jonathan Wonham for his very generous patronage
of our press; as well as our other patrons and investors who wish to remain
anonymous.*

*American spelling and usage is employed in this collection by decision of
the translator.*

WWW.EYEWEARPUBLISHING.COM

HESTER KNIBBE is one of the most acclaimed contemporary poets in the Netherlands. The author of fifteen collections of poems and the recipient of numerous national awards, her most recent books include *Oogsteen*, a selected poems published in 2009, and *Archaïsch de dieren* (2014) for which she won the VSB Poetry Prize.

JACQUELYN POPE is the author of *Watermark* (Marsh Hawk Press). Her poems and translations have been published widely in the US and UK. She is the recipient of a 2015 NEA Translation Fellowship, a PEN/Heim Translation Fund grant, and awards from the Academy of American Poets and the Massachusetts Cultural Council.

Table of Contents

Introduction — 9

It is the eye my love — 11

Deceptive Days
A Deceptive Day — 14
Last Night — 21
The Stone — 22
Delphi — 23
Standing — 24
Michelangelo's Pietà — 25
A Robe of Flesh — 26
Mirrorwoman — 27
Glasswork — 28

The Flexibility of Stone
The Archeologist — 30
The Flexibility of Stone — 31
Underway — 32
Persephone — 33
Demeter — 34
Orpheus — 35
Eurydice — 36
Zijnstra Inc. — 37

Letter from Pompei
The River — 40
Letter from Pompei — 41

Disturbed Ground
After the Flood — 50
Lava and Sand — 51
Psalm 4631 — 52
Oder — 53

The Son — 54
Search — 57
Homecoming — 58

Thetis' Heel
Law — 60
Thetis' Heel — 61
Postcard — 62
Living, Leaving — 63
Body & Co. — 65
Sleep — 66
Light-years — 67

Having a Place
Habitat — 70
Voyage — 71
Tree — 72
Hungerpots — 73
Having a Place — 74
Destination — 77
Baucis Counts Down — 78

Archaic the Animals
And they said that — 80
Pro domo — 81
Wean — 88
Acquittal for Cain — 93
Yes — 95
There is Always — 96

Notes — 104
Acknowledgements — 105

Introduction

Born in 1946 in Harderwijk, The Netherlands, Hester
Knibbe has lived in Rotterdam since 1972, where she worked
for many years as a clinical pharmaceutical analyst and was
the director of a hospital pharmacy. Her first collection
of poems was published in 1982; since that time she has
published fourteen more collections of poetry. Knibbe has
garnered both public and critical acclaim and has received
numerous national literary awards: her most recent book,
Archaïsch de dieren (Archaic the Animals) received the VSB
Poetry Prize, awarded in January 2015. Knibbe's work has
also been recognized with the Herman Gorter Prize in 2000,
the Anna Blaman Prize in 2001, and the Adriaan Roland
Holst prize in 2009. In addition, Knibbe was named poet
laureate of the city of Rotterdam in 2015.

    Hester Knibbe's poetry is grounded in classical
themes and situations, but these are given a twist. What is
typically thought to be eternal is undermined, reconfigured,
interrupted, while the ephemeral is extended, at least for the
length of a poem. These strategies amplify our notions of
time, history, and of life and death. Throughout her work
she has cast and recast grief, often drawing connections
between ages and cultures. Grief is unfortunately a familiar
source for her, and many of her poems have movingly
addressed the death of her son, his absence, and his vividly
felt presence. In the world conjured by Knibbe's poems there
is an embrace of the fact that things are not always what they
seem. Sometimes they juxtapose emblems of permanence
with transience, or with simple human pettiness, itself a
reminder of our fragility.

    Knibbe twists myths and even the simple
observations of tourists into layered structures of language
that express essential human fears and longing. Mythical
figures speak in these poems, but so do rivers, rocks, and
fountains. There may be a wrenching turn toward the

ominous, but the poems will almost always present the paradox that even, perhaps especially, enduring things are fragile. Time is always slipping past, and change is both constant and inescapable. It is the threat of change, the moment of change, the consequences of change that Hester Knibbe tries to grasp and shape in her poetry as she explores the many lines and shadows between the worlds of life and death, the present and the past.

Jacquelyn Pope
Chicago, USA
June 2015

It is the eye my love
that large or small never sets
the soul behind its lashes, no, it sees. From black

to white the world slips through your lens
into the blind and turns to colors there, to red
and violet, to sea and green and man or thing. It is

the distance, love, for which your arm's
too short, your hand's too small and still
it breezes in and stays

makes your body what it craves.

Deceptive Days

A Deceptive Day

It began that day with so much
blue that the sun shone. A golden
beetle dropped from the sky and we found
a dog on the beach, made of wood,
the mangy kind that you'd kick
away. Black and white, he lay stubbornly sleeping. That

morning we swam out deeper, that afternoon
we climbed a mountain. There was a whiteness
in the light that hardened in photos, extracted
all color from the shadows. In the evening

returned to the murmur of water and
men who leafed through their lives
under jet plane trees, we witnessed
the heavens fade and the mountains far away
conceal their little flaws behind something
with the scent of reverie. Wind

dissolved in the air, swallows began
sieving mosquitoes, they flew the shards
of the day together and women in
their Sunday heels clasped

their bags. There was no evening
paper, so no one had to read
about war again, a golden
beetle dropped from the sky and someone
came by, bent by gout and life
who greeted us: Peace.

All was in full bloom in those days. Pimpernel
and vetch conspired all over the place, growth
had split the stone that was part of the wall,
and we strolled across it.

Below, a blue-lipped sea whined
persistently, we glided to it, our soles
rasping stone after stone: suns
had fallen into the water and were flung

on the shore at night. But we told each other that we could not
carry the weight of all the stones of the world
on our backs, crammed between the clothes
in our bags and that we

shouldn't take on the empty weight of dreams
that would not, should not be stowed under our skulls. We would

take just one and just a few more, at home laying them
at his shoulders among the ones we took from other places.

We kneeled, made ourselves small to see
how they get it done: racing into a traffic jam,
nowhere a collision or delay. And then
at random on the highway a huge roundabout, tunnels
open to both streams: ready to gulp them down.

How do you, the ant, escape the trap?

By feigning cold, carefully
closing up your cramped cocoon, feet held stiff
and close beside you, never even considering
the thought *there is always, but always*
jostling on the way to a somewhere

we end up bent far over. Even
those with enough guts to jog away in time,
aberrantly over the roadside, won't get duped
by distance and the ones before, will escape
the trap for a time, perhaps.

Protector, that he's always been, he is

alone with his herd and autumn
sneaks out of the ground and into leaf
while you could have said, summer

is still white-hot. Gradually sits
more often, looks for support from trees
tall or small, straightens his back, bark
against bark. Asks himself

nothing about darkness or light or why
the contented cattle in his field of vision
cover up so much of the horizon. Sees

enough of shifting, downtime
and milky way. Knows what it is to be naked,
still has the heat of the heavens, but

the chill of the earth
seizes his bones, furrows his skin, eats him
up, little by little.

They saw the fire at night
the wakened children, the men and women
with light in their fingers. Got up

once again. With careful hands
he spreads a sweet thought for the birds
crumbles cake into an early

high tea for the sparrows. She'd rather look
out over the sea than in mirrors now,
looks so often and so far that it settles in her, that

you can see. And as evening comes they feed
silence together, the wine in their glasses twinkles
with the ripe bouquet of a certain summer, a certain then. That

they don't say, but behind their backs nostalgia
whines its peculiar song
while right in front of their noses

another day shrinks toward the smoldering
horizon, line under.

She lay there, still young, still almost
a girl. That she remains. She was

laid on her left side since she was meant
to sleep until her sheet and pillowcase rotted away
and longer still, at least until after Christ. And then

she refused to get up. She lies there
like a lid on her own remains plus what
disappeared – you know how that goes. She lies there
to cover an era and to represent it.

In her right hand a scale. Is she asking
for a pittance of life or eternity? Is she offering
something of her death? Is it edible?
How long does memory stay chewable?

We sat with the beginnings
of calm in our limbs, freed of stories, wine in our glasses,
heard the reluctant sound of some animals: a sow
gathering her young with grunts, the high
screech of an owl and the answer he sought,

plumed and waiting. Meanwhile the sparrows
had left their privet hangout, one wandered alone
in the valley, small, easily trampled. The wind
could be held back with one hand and a little later above
the mountains the pizza margarita moon changed clothes,
to an oh-so-great bare mozzarella.

This is what peace looks like, said the eater.

I thought: *Almost a yellow tune? — Soon*
a storm will come racing off the mountain ridge, drive
into the discos below, rage against shutters,
shatter glass — naturally, the bottle
appears to be empty — soon

someone will coolly close the view, flip
open the gate, kick us out of the courtyard.

Last Night

Saved two children last night.
They lay under thin black ice
one gone blue, the other grey.
I laid them out on grass
that snapped under my step
wrung their bodies warm and dry
gave them the gust of my breath.

Then I looked out at the morning
that lay lukewarm on the water
put on a tank top
arranged some grasses in a vase
fished two children out of sleep.

The Stone

Last night I had a house on a hill, around it
a model garden. In the garden lay

a gigantic stone, length twice
its width. Like a baptismal font, a sloppy
star with a mouth. I walked

through the garden, kept my distance, looked
away from it. Then it stood up, destroying
the beds and the lawn as it clambered after me

up the hill. Go away, I said or
hide in a cupboard if you have to, I
have guests coming and a moving stone

will put them off. I belong to this house
it responded, so let me stay, sit
on the sofa with the guests. Don't worry,

a stone speaks softly and only for itself,
doesn't interrupt or irritate. And if you
don't want me I'll make myself bigger, break

open and become a fountain, one that can be seen
from far away. Not a lovely one with fans and mists
but one raining hail and flinging stones.

Delphi

The gate stands open and the path upward
has been studded with superstition and sun. We
strap on bag and camera. The thin
sand that plaits itself into skins leaves

the spot with us. We got here
by memory and tarnished hope:
there'd be temples, high-sounding hymns.

Remnants of stone ordered in the array of death
bluntly set us straight: neither god nor
muse is praised, Apollo has vanished.
Someone has roped that loss off.

Tall, blonde, bronzed – that's the way I pictured him,
I say. You laugh, wander off where
an indistinct arch blends you into antiquity.

And for a moment you alter the centuries,
become the player who just left me,
you play the oldest, cruelest
game: *I love you I love you not*.

Standing

Turned to stone I stand on this earth
in a long skirt and a shawl
that he pinned close across my breasts
because the world insists on it.
That's how I was raised.

My eyes have neither iris nor pupil
so I look to the inside, want to hear
there everything that happens outside.

From what I observe a smile
lies frozen around my lips
that just keeps freezing. Thaw me
adorn me with a cap of blooms
and long stalks in my body.

Michelangelo's Pietà

Died for a belief and became a new one
at the same time. She'd never wanted that, it was

not why she'd borne a child. Still she does not cover him,
simply holds him on her lap: *grown*

body dear to me. Perhaps he too
was tired of the whole conceit, women

who claimed him and men who would not
credit him. Just died,

neither lamb nor shepherd, to lie
still in the marble of a mother.

A Robe of Flesh

Black tail of winter, it freezes it
cracks around thinning ice. I lug between life
and death, haul her up while she

sinks back sobbing. Break
that ice off your body, I shriek, wake
up, summer could be here at any

moment. Warmth enough to come
for that robe around your bones. Just keep it
together for awhile. A chill has come to dwell in your life.

Mirrorwoman

She wears a mirror on her head
in which she cages her surroundings
but who she is she cannot see:
the form that renames her a woman
she evades with the mirror on

her head. She wears a mirror
in her hair that is steamed up
with turquoise: pickled copper toxin
that erases the face of anyone
fishing for their reflection. She

has adorned herself with a crown
of fresh images in her head
since what that thing sees, she
sees too, all the while her hand
arranges a skirt pleat. She bears

the mirror on her head, snares
in it the Medusa's head of time
and cycles: for centuries
she has artfully distracted the eye
from the sight of her decay.

Glasswork

my love who shelters in his words
sometimes falls silent for a sudden eternity
breathes that silence into a bell of glass
in which he calms storms

he draws lee lines in what was
it's more like a firefirm crackling
when he takes up words with ease
in a single glance, caressing my body

I read him day and night. What will it be like
when he withdraws into the word *old,*
arranges a last room, silver-white,
pushes the furniture a bit closer together

and crams still more fragile glass inside –
what will it be like when he grows transparent and breaks

The Flexibility of Stone

The Archeologist

In one who doesn't speak the story petrifies,
gets stumbled over, causes hurt. Then,

says the man who should know about the past, then
is a word you need to learn now. Then

lived lives had has
a name a body, sacrificial hands

so god might help us. Feel with your hands and feet
back along these countless steps and hear

the incessant bloodrush, its dark red

presence. That was what the man insisted,
in so many words, pointing to the ornate

temple corridor, an altar
conjured at its vanishing point.

The Flexibility of Stone

Take a column consisting
of three slim pillars: a triangle
whose corners have disappeared. Take

several of them and set them in a square
so the middle makes a courtyard where
day and night can live. In the blackest

night of the century the courtyard
wobbles when one column starts to move,
rigid, shyly crossing one leg
behind another, which behind
which can't be said – or no,

the one moves its slim figure
in a dance of supplication around two, making
three have to move his foot

a sloppy fraction. Only their heads
come together still, making a fixed
thought chiseled on a single capital.

Underway

Under the street hangs the ceiling
of the platform we stand
upon. Together we travel
underground – how light it is

going through blackness. No hint
of night and there's nothing of day
to be seen. We are
the quietest passengers – only

the racing carriages. And racing
too what passes us: windows inlaid
with shadows, faces like fossils so
everlastingly underway.

Persephone

He didn't kidnap me: I
was curious, went down
on my own and let myself be taken, pure.
So immortal death came to dwell

with us. My mother cannot grasp that,
she only wants me to dance
for the reapers at the harvest festival,
summer in my head

and in my hair. But I have
a wintry side as well, one that digs
down to the roots, goes in search
of the germ in seed. That

doesn't clash with what's above:
I want to show the sources
of sustenance, what has to fall
at harvest time. To that I have been matched.

Demeter

My child goes missing, turns up time
and time again. She let herself be led
to darkness, no matter how much
I said: no god can be trusted. I too

slept with a god, breaking
the parental ban, but stood with both feet
on the ground: there was a child
to be fed, wood in the hearth,

corn pushing up earth. My daughter
is a child no longer, she's a woman
who can't be kept at home in winter:
the colder it gets here, the further

she withdraws from the fire. But
at the first thaw she returns
and with swift feet she dances
sweet fruit from the earth.

Orpheus

We sank down into
our body: one form
that cannot be split
only riven and missed.

My name must go
obediently with you, my
dearest loss. Our heart
is the lyre in which song

lies defeated and dumb. How
awkwardly we stand here
laden with sorrow and laden
with all the centuries I cried don't

leave my side and then
I had to turn to see.

Eurydice

He set his song on me
fingered the lyre the way he once
touched my skin while I

stiffen with cold. Set aside
under time's scale I live a life
of supplication: Eurydice,

come out! Sepulchral stone and divine bans:
he plays them aside, seduces death
to sleep, then he's let in

and I'm given away, a dowry
to Memory. But life lived

backwards causes harm. Don't look
at what was, darling, look
how I lapse in time
lying there at your feet.

Zijnstra Inc.

In love everything is possible. You doggedly
paper a tree with roses
and say: this was the place
and everyone who passes should

know it. Or someone decides: this deadweight
can't be lifted any longer, I'll set it
like stone at the foot of the cliff, but
it doesn't make walking or breathing

any easier. The asphalt that bridges the river
points up high, the radio
sings *Ach* and *Oh* and on the truck
in front of me, shamelessly written

in the day's filth, it says *Now that you're no longer here*
you're closer than ever before. Exactly so. Who
had the guts, with a single finger in dust, to clear
the way for the most faithful? Soon

the bridge will open, the row will set forth
in obedient motion and I'll pass
the purified sludge of Zijnstra Inc.
and a declaration of love written in mud.

Letter from Pompei

The River

What lies low I fill up with my passing
and through town and country I drag along
a past meant to sink in my depths.

Whether I narrow now or
swell, I whet and wear away the insides
of my skin; I am my bed

and yet I am not. I have
no eye for left or right, drifting
slowly on my underflow, arms
stretched in places to the side, so I take

up still more ground, drowning
just as I extend. Not that I
smother myself – heights
I find there, and also silt.

Letter from Pompei

I.

We went through a narrow passage
just wide enough for two,
and came out in what had been
a city, a drawn out, worn out body.

In its heart the remnants
of gods, around those what moved
when it lived, every roof a hole
to heaven. Around the city

a wall full of silence remains,
inside it time has yet to find its voice,
tossing and turning slowly in its sleep
the way land shifts under the sea.

2.

Enough dust-covered belief here,
enough everyday life polished

smooth. The walls teach us how long
one can endure: one dance

and some fleeting love in plenty of space
and never enough time. Even

as your life, drawn in color,
remains through the ages, smooth,

held to the light it slowly lightens you
a dance, a love lighter.

3.

Almost nothing fits completely in the shell
of its word: war, for instance,
is too big and disaster too is tight.

A city like this fits its skin
so closely, you know that nothing
has disappeared, and if after years

you hack a shaft to that hidden
past, as you hack you'll feel
the past already

sticking. Then when you land unexpectedly
in a furnished house, bump
blindly into a wall, you scratch out

sweet longings, naked and harrowing.
You clean them

and put a plaster
here and there.

4.

Imagine that, while the day
capsizes, while fire rushes out of the mountain,
imagine that the child inside you just then
moves and descends.

And you cry out
with all your mouths: no
don't do that, but you do
have to push and you push

an angel into hell. Never
is an umbilical cord cut off forever.

5.

A skeleton is stubborn.

How they did it: filled up a hole,
plastered bones and chipped a person
out of his youngest moment.

But no one had enough god
in their lungs to make him move
again. What I

displace in air in this lightcask
I push aside for just a moment:
like a living

about-face from the solidified
I stroll around, my eye on
what might spare me in
a coming thousand-year void.

Layers of wasted earth
crowd around before, around
after: stiff buckled
body, dying to remain.

6.

Peeled away by time
an uninhabitable city remains. Every house

beheaded, heart and gods
plundered, still the walls stand
enchanted with the marks

of their tenants. Permeated
by earth, they've remained. Their legacy
is dust on my feet,
dirt under my nails.

7.

An overcast blue peace wraps around
the ancient, dewy-eyed love
strolls by temple and house.

And we're there too, hand in hand,
prepared for the consolation
of silence, so that just for a moment
it becomes deserted in our heads.

With so much faded death around us it seems good
to live slowly. *Andante un poco
sostenuto* I hum, walking over the stones.

Disturbed Ground

After the Flood

After the Flood there you sit
next to the boat, the fish
gasping for air, the hare finding
nothing to eat yet and all the birds

left behind. There you sit
in the same skirt in which, waters ago,
you boarded the ship, but the dance
has drained from your feet. For once the rain

blew over at last, the water
was lulled mirror-smooth, you saw

your world turned upside down and lower still
any movement stalled for good and
when you took a better look that too
that image stayed with you and how

with each glance your essence
lost more depth. Now you sit,
ram and ewe already on dry ground,
all at sea in flotsam and jetsam.

Lava and Sand

The soil I'm walking over comes

from deeper: a fire had done it in,
a stewpot had suddenly popped
and its contents streamed
out wave over wave until
it reached the water, until the sea
called it a day and struck back

with a counterwave. Stony nightblack
dreambarren land where tawny
thyme wrestles up and thistle is stitched
to every bare thing. Over this malevolence
I carry you in me,
sevenmonths deadchild, out to the sea

Psalm 4631

In my need I call out
to nothing and to no one, I am silent. One who's
seen dust gone to dust and bygones and survives

has forgotten how to cry. Let the oak moan
and groan about leaves fallen
too early to the ground, the branch

torn off its trunk. Let me stand wordless
in its shadow. Let

my silence be not small and stooped
but worthily high
and broad as the crown of the tree

now its roots and silence
are fastened to him and prayer
is smothered in the ground.

Oder

This is the waterfront you walked along
whistling a new spring song, walking
hand in hand with your love. Same banks

but the water isn't, that water
is long gone and what grew then

has blown over. The land lends air
to desolation. This is the waterfront

where you whistled – past tense, the horizon
is tainted with your death, winter
just won't get out

of what the cow parsley brushes aside.

The Son

My mother sits at the table, writing
inconsolably. So I don't console
her. She doesn't want to lose me. While

I sit next to her, she looks
just past me, finding the white
under her hands that she fills

with me. My mother listens
to what no one can see: me, talking
to her again as we sit

together on the verge of the garden, doors
opened on a new
season. My mother

can hear me, she
listens, I speak:

★

While I still had a life to be
lived, I was tackled by the heaviest

sleep, a cold haze I can't wake from,
no matter how you call to me
in silence, beg for me to exist once more

in circling blood. You fit me
with my voice and skin and hair and once again
I walk whistling down the street, but when you

wake and your dreams are gone, you sit
by me again in my wintertime.

★

I knew this and I
said it to you, too: the earth

you borrow to give weight
to your body you
must give back when
at last you

hover over your very own

being. But when daylight
left my life for the last
time, it was almost as difficult
as my very

first beginning — *mama* —
that I've forgotten

Search

Wandered tonight through a city
as ruined as a body with broken
ribs and a bared heart. Looked for you

there with cookies in my pocket, searched
for a sigh, for movement in demolished
streets and alleys. Tonight

since I'd forgotten for a moment where you are,
I searched for you with hope in my bones.
But no matter how I lured you with my voice
and my eyes, walls of debris

grew up steadily around you, cellars seemed
to creep around you. I remained alone
with those cookies in my pocket
and kept calling and walking.

Homecoming

I dreamed that I dreamed
of you: we sat on the sofa
and talked a while, you wore the sweater I'd
worn that day, your hair was
wet from all the rain. Your body, solid

and warm, was once again as fresh
as when you'd been down in the fen
and you recounted animatedly
how different beyond turned out to be,
how deep the roots
of the oak went down. And I

told you what I'd experienced
up here, how the hazel
had grown. And what a year
for spiders, I said. You burst out laughing.

Thetis' Heel

Law

Take water, evident, that feeds the seas
or wind that blows and turns apathetically,
the grass that grows and once again gets
mowed, or us, growing larger at first,
then shrinking wrinkling simplifying
to nothing: always changing. Or

more capriciously: you'll get from A to Z, but then
– just about at J – suddenly fate stands
in your way and takes you off. Where to?

The water shacked up with seas knows.
The wind that leaves no trace knows.
The grass stutters it out under the blade.

Thetis' Heel

Even gods, though they were born
in our own heads, died out to myth.

Just as no one can point to the source
of the spring or later at sea can say: this

is the water from deep in the earth, that
flowed from the mountaintops, so

is the stream of mortals and gods.

About my origins I know
nothing. I married the earth, a child

grew in me, fell
out of me at last, and I

babbled: little mutt of mine, I'll
name you, dunk you in invulnerability.

He smiled at me, held me tightly
by the heel and said *mama*.

Postcard

You were there. The glossy card
depicts what you described: a world
so vast that it slides from all four sides
of the card – just like the way you

disappeared from the landscape: wanderer
who simply stepped across
the horizon. The world on the card is significant

only for the way you look at us, word for word,
backwards. But your handwriting
has faded too, the light of day steals
the nightblue ink of your pen. As if you

must be read in increasing quiet,
in order to hear, perhaps,
how you read it out loud.

Living, Leaving

I have to straighten up the attic, the rooms
the whole collection kept for years
for a later I no longer have
can now be done away with. But *keep it*

lies waiting, grinning: shards
that fit a memory, sleeping bags,
backpacks with sand from vacations,
skates, the imprint of feet

in shoes. In dusty drawers scratchpad,
diary, school notebook, calligraphy pad
nagging to be read, rustled through softly.

But hardest of all are the boxes with
folded paper, stories and drawings of labyrinths,
worlds that have been lost.

His room retains what it has:
the view stands etched the same way
in the windows, on the shelves the books
support each other, backs turned to the reader

who disappeared. The abandoned dresser
stands sadly broad, it holds
the big deposit. Keep off! the drawers
stick, he lives here in manuscripts, names

and cards; he entrusted us with
what must be preserved, favorites
large and small, secret knowledge
that adds to it. We contain much

more than things alone
since everything is finished.

Body & Co.

The gulls have none of this heaviness, they
fly with purpose, even their bobbing
is vital – head into the wind –
and the cat's laziness takes on
a regal sense once her purring begins.

A list of 'things to do.' Begin
I command, but my body complains that it
craves something else, the newspaper
a walk because the head
the head – How do I get

this done what's over the horizon
and hidden deeper still, how do I dig myself
into that cradle and casket so some sense
becomes clear, how will I ever tame
the dead mess that rages

in me. No, none of this trouble
sounds in the gull's cries.

Sleep

If sleep was a father
who comforted, pulled up covers and whispered

go wake him up, turn back the stone
at his head and say, it's

spring, you should get up
again, if you opened

your eyes then, yawning, dusting
the earth from you, let me sleep then, sleep
keep me covered, tucked in.

Light-years

It's a beautiful world, you said,
with these trees, marshes, deserts,
grasses, rivers and seas

and so on. And the moon is really something
in its circuits
of relative radiance. Include

the wingèd M, voluptuous
Venus, hotheaded Mars, that lucky devil
J and cranky Saturn, of course, plus

U and N and the wanderer P, in short
the whole solar family, complete with its
Milky Way, and count up all the other

systems with dots and spots and in
that endless emptiness what you've got
is a commotion of you-know-what. It's a beautiful

universe, you said, just take a good look
through the desert's dark glasses
for instance or on your back

in seas of grass, take a good look
at the deluge of that Rorschach – we're standing out there
somewhere, together.

Having a Place

Habitat

Very old people lived in that city.
They mopped the streets with dragging feet, supported
by canes and rolling walkers, tottered around
in cafés, desolately eating their cake. In that city

there lived some very old people. Sometimes
you'd see two arm-in-arm, holding each other upright
with a tenderness so natural that it
looked like they were whispering *stay a little*

longer, stay a little longer, but they were hushed,
silent, mostly because if they had to move
their legs there wasn't enough breath left
to speak. In that city lived many

who leaned into their end, who belonged to the pattern
of pavement and facades, the endless weighing
and measuring, lines limits lapses, squares and alleys
moving heaven and earth, a bench in the sun.

Voyage

He is in a photograph, standing
next to me; my time lies locked away

in his eyes. We watch the unloading
of the boat, rough Playmobil
that fights with its moorings. Like this,

in the shelter of a body, I feel
myself untethered, come
what may: empty landscape

with a tent that makes the earth
a bare mattress and where we break our
daily bread with every weapon at hand,

or a luxury room with a canopy bed,
the Last Supper in cross stitch on the wall.

Tree

No twig or knob points to what comes,
its branches wide as if in reproach, it's been given
to woodpeckers beetles and mold. Something

at its base, in the subsoil, the yard
too wet, a rat or a worm gnawing at
the roots, rot that breaks off

the flow of sap. No spring
to be found in it. Dying
keeps it in wintry form and storm

undresses it step by step. It's already missing
fingers hand a wrist, but on an arm
of its skeleton the turtledoves have settled in.

Hungerpots

Did an argument break out in the kitchen that morning?
Was there smashing of pots and pans: you
want to eat somewhere else? Go on,

get out! Or were they set outside, shrewd,
meant to feed on dust and hunger or to tempt the doves
of peace? Nothing wrong with that as long as
the cook stays put by another fire. Hollow

vessels on grass socks, what do they want from this
puzzle of trees and clouds? Even the wind
seems to have forgotten how to whistle and wherever
you look, those who are gone cannot be seen.

They're steeped to their lips in bronzed silence. O
let their bellies chime like clocks, whack
with ladles and sticks, drive devilish
death out of those pots!

Having a Place

1.

One day the image you have of yourself
no longer corresponds to what you see in the mirror.

In it stands someone you recognize
as the person you are, but looking as if a jet

sleep had come over it and a winter in which
it was white and silent and afterward

came rain, a storm hung
to dry under the heavens. That

shrinks in your mirrored face. In your head
lives an image from last summer, but now you

face another season, you have to line your eyes
again, do something with your lips, revise yourself.

2.

One day the one you fell in love with has disappeared.
You live in the same house and you care about each other,

sure, but another kind of tenderness
is needed to break through to each other and

sometimes a reticence sits down to dinner
that is difficult to talk around.

Not that the bodies don't speak to each other,
they still stroke and touch every Eden, explore

every heaven, but there are also small
torn stitches in the seam of love, invisible

in mirrors, because it had to drag itself
across the earth, catching on twigs and stones.

3.

One day you are out strolling on ebbland
and suddenly stumble over its space.

A stoical sea underlies it, wind
creating a haze that obscures the smudgy stacks

under the heavens and in the distance stands
a leadblue graphic, cardiogram of the stones,

extending massively, light forgotten
once again. Nothing here that reflects you. Sand

seeps from under your feet,
where you stand slowly fills

with sucking water: this is
your place now, tomorrow this was your place.

Destination

As we rode into the village we came upon
a convergence of old customs: there was
an empty house and the door stood wide open.

The men from the village lugged a cupboard into the house.
The men from the village hauled a table into the house.
The men from the village heaved a bed into the house.

And the women of the village bore
dishes and plates and glasses and something to
make the bed habitable into the house.

Then the men pushed a son inside.
Learn to light a fire, they said,
learn to put out a fire, they said,
we're latching the shutters.

Then the women pushed a daughter inside.
Learn to be hot, they said,
learn to be cold, they said,
we're barricading the door.

Baucis Counts Down

I must strip myself from the wooden woman. First
chop away all the branches, then laboriously
step out of her bark, and now my love's

set free. Bent, we shuffle into the temple
devoted to love and sacrifice ourselves
to time, until its golden roof
collapses, is replaced by

leaf and twig: a hut that makes the flood
look lower now. The gods stand
at our side. Back to that shelter, to
a meager meal prepared with care, god

by god glides into a stranger's skin, disappears
into the desert once he knocks. Now
we are alone again, in poverty that
seems bearable, the children

already gone. My love lies
with me more often, his skin
growing slowly smooth, as do I. And the grey
disappears from our hair and voices come

closer, though they are recognizable
from far away. The door swings
shut. There is a child who wants to go on
and another child who strips herself from me.

Archaic the Animals

And they said that

a blessing means help, but that night
there were so many wounds on the world that my
eyes went dim and my legs lame. And I was

afraid afraid of blood on my hands and
that I'd go around with it over my face belly
and arms. That's why I cried out

bless me, bless me the terrified.

Pro domo

It was hot in paradise, the plants
panted for water, the lion lay knocked out
with the lamb and slept. It all needed

to be pruned weeded mowed, but we had
no word yet for weed shovel lopper
scythe. Still, water streamed across

the garden from somewhere and to elsewhere
and we ate leafgreens, carrots, plucked the fruit
– how it could ripen! – the cherries delicious

we spit their pits on the ground and
seedlings sprouted. So there had to be

more under the sun, something
you might call beginning and end.

We never asked for it
but doubt seeped in: had we
been given brains so as not to want

to know? Then a storm tracked through the garden,
crossed right through us and made us
aware of our bodies and of

each other. The animals awoke too growled
suddenly knew a sound for *danger!*

So it was the wind that destroyed
the shelter in which we lived, a tornado
that picked us up smacked us down in love-hate. We

acquired a dark kind of power and thoughts that
whirled and stabbed like flames in our chests.
Had we asked for this?

All those words we got there: anger
fear wish envy slaughter hunger slave
master whore hagiography dirty sick time
pregnant eternal windbag sword scourge

and nostalgia, not to be forgotten. And with them
mercy and healing. We must

make space for the futile, for gross flaws,
and for imperfections, we said
and we need to keep together,
cherish each other. We learned to seek

to avoid each other, simplicity plurality
vanity. We grew stooped, that too

was part of the omniscience we unwillingly
took on. And we knew our stupidity.

We cradled a child and it cried.
We suckled it then and it sucked and sucked
the earth inside. In its head

more and more there grew thoughts
of why and what and – There

were words like want and not. There
were actions and little could be said

against this or that. There
was talk of a chain of people: that one and

that one and me too a little. There was
a hiatus in *knowing for sure*. One thought

collapsed and then another.

We sought to find a place to sleep
and to stay, had the kind of body

that wanted a place, something
of its own at least two arm-spans wide.

Around our necks the currency of fear, a noose
of loss took our breath. We had
stupid destructive thoughts that we couldn't

stow away, that provoked us
smirking, kept pointing to us. So it was

that we turned around chased away called names
knocked teeth out of jeering mouths.

Our mistake? That we consisted
of a body, were hungry, drowned

our thirst. We should have been simply
breath, exhaled air and that

we became in the end. Our misstep
was that we sought a way out, always

searching but as soon as we found it
we had to leave. That's why

we rebelled against the unwieldy principle
of whoever is first, shall be. We were
the ones never allowed to join.

Loneliness became a voice
that spoke to us, got those eyes. *Do it*
said the voice *despite your softness you were
made for destruction.* The eyes

blinked that it had to be and that afterward
we would sleep like a baby. Searched

in books, made a plan and wrote a prophecy
of what the world has in excess

what it lacks and that only a verdict
that cuts away and frays forever
can heal. Blew all on our lonesome

ruin throughout the land so
they would know of us so they would know.

Wean

*

Never housed in picture frames: took suitcases
lodged my little ones in them. They were
too alive for strangers' eyes, too loud
for the silence that was expected

around me. I saved them prematurely
from pestering, deathtrap, being smacked
out of balance, because this is certain:
lion and lamb are no longer together. I bore

technicality after technicality, declared inadmissible, a
brief gasping for air while my breasts engorged
no mother no mother no

began to leak. Afraid, I longed
to latch on to necessity.

★★

But I couldn't get rid of them, that's why
I kept them in the suitcases.

Because it's not like something you wear
on the outside, a T-shirt
pants you get tired of or wear out and

it's not something like nails
or hair that you cut off either: what you carried

inside you you don't want to lose. So
those suitcases meant a sort of trip back to
another uterine darkness. What did they need

with light in their closed eyes.

2.

If I'd been a sea animal, with more than
seven tentacles, I'd have had no hesitation
would have fanned the stuff off them so they

could breathe. But I had to make do with just
one heart some brains and these two hands.

I have cherished foddered fed them with
thoughts of later, but something in them didn't want
to grow, went clumsily wrong. Bathwater

too hot or too cold, wrong socks on? Too little
or too much cuddling close, tender hair
cut too short or braided too tight?

Though they didn't want to, they must and they should,
I scolded and forced them to be happy though I knew well
the way life sometimes – Slave's work, forced labor.

3.

Big as he was, a giant child,
he sat in a car and did not listen, had
strange wrong clothes on and the wind
increased, but he didn't listen,

with a slow old man's hand he pulled
an idiotic checkered pointed hood
over his blank amazement,
didn't see his mother's panic

when she called: a storm is coming.
He just sat there all too little afraid
too coarsely built for a child's car: clay

doll over six feet tall that
out of breath I breathed into life.

4.

Sleep just sleep in your spectrum of silence
the trees will give you shade
weave a gauze of coolness over you
and everything holds its breath.

      – Mama the birds sing so somberly here
      a black seasonless summer reigns
      a huge an enormous scattering blossoms

Your sunny smile is in the photo
your beautiful smile is in the photo

Acquittal for Cain

the son

Guilt is an agreement. Despite
all the homesick stories our parents told
of how peace oh peace looks, he had
to snatch and slaughter the lamb

to elevate himself. The heavens, higher and stronger than
any of the gods created on earth, are my witness.

Ashen remains + smoke adrift with mumbled prayers

from which not even a syllable lingered.
Sacrifice: a life for a thought.

Thought: is there a promise hidden
in death? Out of compassion I, his keeper,
shall release him from his meager condition
on this earth.

the mother

What he knew about it? Death

is something you can imagine but never really
know. Of course we set

traps and snares, gulleted and ate
the defenseless beasts, but

that a human being would lie there, so still in his
lonesome body, was much too –
                                    One
had to come first, but we
taught them ourselves how to slay, flay

to quell hunger or for an extra skin
over back shoulders and nakedness, we taught them

how to prepare a sacrifice for some security
in and after this life. All the while we

knew very well what peace looks like. Fury
is a fashion in this post-Eden and there is

always something that wants to throw us away
just when we think we are settling in.

Of our own mortality we knew
almost nothing. Neither did he.

Yes

Love, yes there is always a body involved
and that makes it and makes it, makes it

tricky sometimes. But it doesn't matter, we've been
together for so long that we've stashed ourselves
inside each other, won't get lost can't get away anymore.

Of course, omens get under the skin, dance along
when you dance, run when you run, hang out

on the sofa too, just sitting there and later Fail
makes off with your dreams, a winter afflicts
the old river that wants to stream. But it

doesn't matter and the sphinx who poses
the riddle *who of who is most* is nothing

to get worked up about, we'll just take each other
by the hand and where the road ends we will sleep.

There Is Always

There is always a first
head that you draw
with two
eyes no
mouth yet
arms and legs no
hands and feet. There is

always a first
mouth that appears
in the slapdash
head without
speaking
though you quickly
learn that

this

is how smiles are drawn
how sadness seems.

Even when the nest
is a mishmash
of chance
findings
the egg gets laid
and breaks
in the end.

What you're after is

not the shell
that protects you
but a frail
brokenness: daring
that movement
without awareness of
repetition boredom

profiles
Facebook

Meanwhile the egg
scratches its happiness and
rightness together,
as the hand belonging to
the slapdash
head
starts an uncompleted

curve: it's time it's time it's

time for études cantatas
aubades quatre-mains
escapades a nimble-fingered
exploration of questions with the whole
body fervently confessing
the complete catechism
of love and

answering: yes
that's why.

There is always a first

doubt: *what for*. Knocked at the gods' door, but
they were not in, had other hassles to manage: grass
that modified, suddenly denigrated its roots wanted no more to do
with them, air was enough for it. I dug and dug in the earth
constantly finding under and under but once exhumed it was
a mountain where each answer every surprise
had to find itself among the others.

Then I went walking in wind and into a light
that did not cease as long as I walked in that light
as long as it skimmed over my earth. It had
no above or below, no left or right, nowhere
a middle, I could not put my hand on it, it laid
itself on my hand and my head and slipped sparkling
from under my feet when I tried to walk over it.

Like a jay bird
setting stores for winter I keep
a stock of snatched moments. In that

photo they are far
stronger than us, power flexes
in their muscles and we stand by like

their begetters: marginal figures

who re-read even now, shut books
search in cupboards for passwords,
who – their heads a woozy place for drifters and the blind – still

know how to crack codes, retrieve
the most fleeting names in a tangle of webs.

Now that the land is being robbed of foliage
the trees stand dressed in their evening wear of bark

the honey sugars and we
scrape summer's fruit from the jam pots

something in us inaudible as snow begins

to loosen. The eye in the slapdash
head, without the burden of hands and feet, finds the way

to the path by the buckthorn, above it
a flight of drunken birds, walks back into a light that

just won't, sees in that light banally prophetic: there is always a final

breach of membrane and shell.

Let us burn

the old letters, watch all the beautiful
rain-drenched sun-bleached words and lines
go up in flames while shamelessly

retaining their contents. We've been
lucky, oh what we've been —
                              Let us

explore other cities, wander through new
streets, past buskers and rough sleepers,
get used to leaving.
                              Let us

eat there and drink and give

the singer enough to get drunk on
the beggar what he deserves.

Notes

'Hungerpots'
'Hungerpots' was written to accompany a work by the
Dutch sculptor Bas Maters. The title is a neologism of the
poet's.

'Baucis Counts Down'
In Ovid's *Metamorphosis*, Baucis and Philemon were an old
married couple who were hospitable to three strangers who
had been turned away from other households, sharing with
them the little food they had. The strangers turned out to
be gods, who had come to earth to study the way humans
behaved. In their judgement, the world of loveless and selfish
humans would have to be destroyed by a flood.

Baucis and Philemon were spared, however, and were
granted a wish. They wished to die at the same time. That
they did: at the end of their lives they were transformed into
two willow trees, standing side by side.

I thought of this myth when I saw *Albero Porta* (Door Tree)
by Giuseppe Penone. He took a thick tree trunk and peeled
back its layers until a young tree with branches was visible –
a tree that was about 25 years old, his own age at the time.
(HK)

'Wean'
The first section of 'Wean' is based on the trial of Sietske
H., a young woman convicted in 2011 of killing four of her
newborn babies.

Acknowledgements

Grateful acknowledgment is made to the editors of the
following journals, in which some of these poems first
appeared: *Asymptote, The Common, The Dark Horse, PN
Review, Poetry, Poetry Daily, Poetry International, Poetry London,
Poetry Northwest, Salamander,* and *Azul* (The Netherlands).

I would like to thank the PEN/Heim Translation Fund
for its vital support of the completion of this work. I am
also deeply grateful for the generous funding provided
by an NEA Translation Fellowship, which helped make
this translation possible. Many thanks to Edwin Smet for
his diligent work on the design of this book. And thanks
especially, as ever, to Don Share.

– JP –

EYEWEAR PUBLISHING

EYEWEAR POETRY

MORGAN HARLOW MIDWEST RITUAL BURNING

KATE NOAKES CAPE TOWN

RICHARD LAMBERT NIGHT JOURNEY

SIMON JARVIS EIGHTEEN POEMS

ELSPETH SMITH DANGEROUS CAKES

CALEB KLACES BOTTLED AIR

GEORGE ELLIOTT CLARKE ILLICIT SONNETS

HANS VAN DE WAARSENBURG THE PAST IS NEVER DEAD

DAVID SHOOK OUR OBSIDIAN TONGUES

BARBARA MARSH TO THE BONEYARD

MARIELA GRIFFOR THE PSYCHIATRIST

DON SHARE UNION

SHEILA HILLIER HOTEL MOONMILK

FLOYD SKLOOT CLOSE READING

PENNY BOXALL SHIP OF THE LINE

MANDY KAHN MATH, HEAVEN, TIME

MARION MCCREADY TREE LANGUAGE

RUFO QUINTAVALLE WEATHER DERIVATIVES

SJ FOWLER THE ROTTWEILER'S GUIDE TO THE DOG OWNER

TEDI LÓPEZ MILLS DEATH ON RUA AUGUSTA

AGNIESZKA STUDZINSKA WHAT THINGS ARE

JEMMA BORG THE ILLUMINATED WORLD

KEIRAN GODDARD FOR THE CHORUS

COLETTE SENSIER SKINLESS

BENNO BARNARD A PUBLIC WOMAN

ANDREW SHIELDS THOMAS HARDY LISTENS TO LOUIS ARMSTRONG

JAN OWEN THE OFFHAND ANGEL

A.K. BLAKEMORE HUMBERT SUMMER

SEAN SINGER HONEY & SMOKE

RUTH STACEY QUEEN, JEWEL, MISTRESS

EYEWEAR PROSE

SUMIA SUKKAR THE BOY FROM ALEPPO WHO PAINTED THE WAR

ALFRED CORN MIRANDA'S BOOK

EYEWEAR LITERARY CRITICISM

MARK FORD THIS DIALOGUE OF ONE - WINNER OF THE 2015 PEGASUS AWARD FOR POETRY CRITICISM FROM THE POETRY FOUNDATION (CHICAGO, USA).